Congressional Research Service

The Smart Grid and Cybersecurity— Regulatory Policy and Issues

Richard J. Campbell
Specialist in Energy Policy

June 15, 2011

Congressional Research Service

7-5700

www.crs.gov

R41886

CRS Report for Congress ——————————

Prepared for Members and Committees of Congress

Summary

Electricity is vital to the commerce and daily functioning of United States. The modernization of the grid to accommodate today's uses is leading to the incorporation of information processing capabilities for power system controls and operations monitoring. The "Smart Grid" is the name given to the evolving electric power network as new information technology systems and capabilities are incorporated. While these new components may add to the ability to control power flows and enhance the efficiency of grid operations, they also potentially increase the susceptibility of the grid to cyber (i.e., computer-related) attack since they are built around microprocessor devices whose basic functions are controlled by software programming. The potential for a major disruption or widespread damage to the nation's power system from a large scale cyberattack has increased focus on the cybersecurity of the Smart Grid.

Federal efforts to enhance the cybersecurity of the electrical grid were emphasized with the recognition of cybersecurity as a critical issue for electric utilities in developing the Smart Grid. The Federal Energy Regulatory Commission (FERC) received primary responsibility for the reliability of the bulk power system from the Energy Policy Act of 2005. FERC subsequently designated the North American Electric Reliability Corporation (NERC) as the "Electric Reliability Organization" (ERO) with the responsibility of establishing and enforcing reliability standards. Compliance with reliability standards for electric utilities thus changed from a voluntary, peer-driven undertaking to a mandatory function. The Energy Independence and Security Act of 2007 (EISA) later added requirements for "a reliable and secure electricity infrastructure" with regard to Smart Grid development. NERC is also responsible for standards for critical infrastructure protection (CIP) which focus on planning and procedures for the physical security of the grid. Self-determination is a key part of the CIP reliability process. Utilities are allowed to self-identify what they see as "critical assets" under NERC regulations. Only "critical cyber assets" (i.e., as essential to the reliable operation of critical assets) are subject to CIP standards. FERC has directed NERC to revise the standards so that some oversight of the identification process for critical cyber assets was provided, but any revision is again subject to stakeholder approval. While reliability standards are mandatory, the ERO process for developing regulations is somewhat unusual in that the regulations are essentially being established by the entities who are being regulated. This may potentially be a conflict of interest, especially when cost of compliance is a concern, and acceptable standards may conceivably result from the option with the lowest costs. Since utility systems are interconnected in many ways, the system with the least protected network potentially provides the weakest point of access.

Cybersecurity threats represent a constantly moving and increasing target for mitigation activities and mitigation efforts could likewise spiral upward in costs. Recovery of costs may present a major challenge especially to distribution utilities and state commissions charged with overseeing utility costs. EISA only requires states to consider recovery of costs related to Smart Grid systems. FERC has jurisdiction over the bulk power grid, and cannot compel entities involved in distribution to comply with its regulations. Recoverability from a cyber attack on the scale of something which could take down a significant portion of the grid will likely be very difficult, but maintaining a ready inventory of critical spare parts in close proximity to key installations could quicken recovery efforts from some types of attack. The electricity grid is connected to (and largely dependent on) the natural gas pipeline, water supply, and telecommunications systems. Technologies being developed for use by the Smart Grid could also be used by these industries. Consideration could be given to applying similar control system device and system safeguards to these other critical utility systems.

Contents

Figures

Contacts

Introduction

Electricity is vital to the commerce and daily functioning of United States. The electrical grid of the United States consists of all the power plants generating electricity, together with the transmission and distribution lines and their associated transformers and substations which bring power to end-use customers. Electric power generation in the United States is currently dominated by the use of combustible fuels, such as coal and natural gas, or from biomass. These fuels are burned to produce steam in boilers which is used to turn turbine-generators which produce electricity. Nuclear power uses heat from the decay of radioactive elements to produce steam. However, electricity can also be generated directly by wind turbines, solar power, geothermal energy, and hydropower. **Figure 1** illustrates the phases of the electric power production process. Electricity from large central station power plants is routed to a step-up transformer which raises the voltage so the power can be sent over high-voltage transmission lines to step-down transformers in substations which then transfer this energy at lower voltages via distribution lines to industrial, commercial, and residential users.

Figure 1. Elements of the Electric Power System

Simplified Schematic

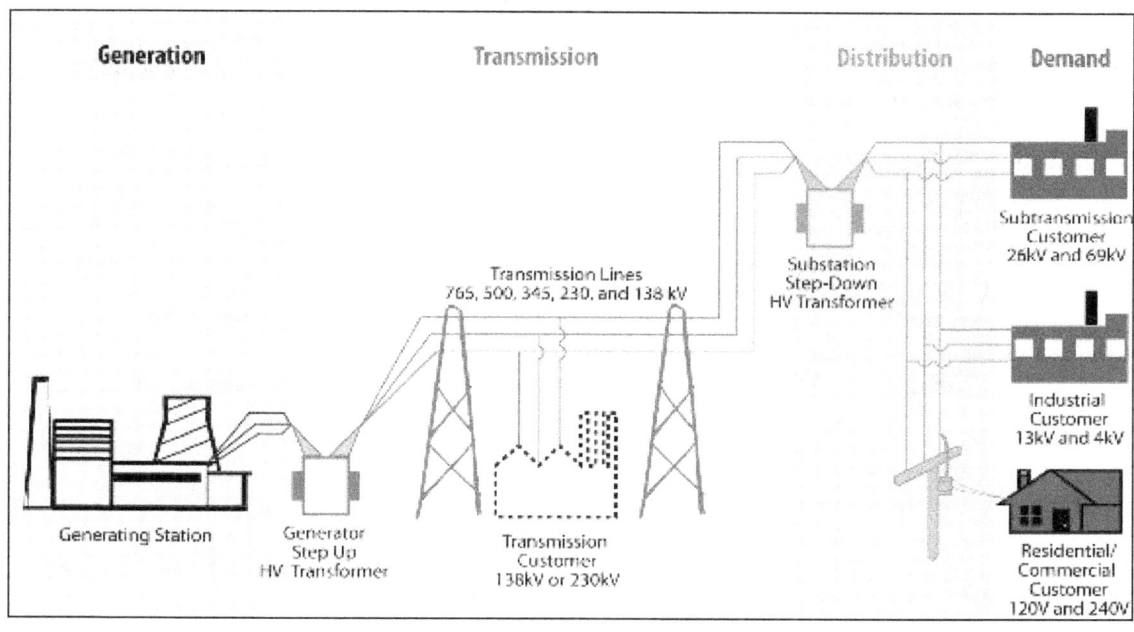

Source: CRS, based on graphic found at https://reports.energy.gov/BlackoutFinal-Web.pdf (p. 5).

Generally, electricity must be used as soon as it is produced because large amounts of electricity cannot be easily stored.

Originally, the individual company systems were not linked, but with greater electricity demand came the necessity of sharing generation resources. This sharing of generation resources required an interconnection of separate company systems to enable power sales and transfers. These aggregated power systems form three major "interconnections"—the Eastern and Western interconnections, and the Electric Reliability Council of Texas which includes most of the state of Texas. Within these interconnections are reliability regions, and a number of balancing authorities[1] which "integrate resource plans ahead of time, maintain load-interchange generation balance" within a balancing authority area, and "support interconnection frequency in real-time."[2] The grid also connects the many publicly and privately owned electric utility and power companies in different states and regions of the United States[3] (and in Canada and Mexico).

Congress passed the Public Utility Regulatory Policies Act of 1978 (P.L. 95-617) which allowed non-utility power producers into wholesale power markets (e.g., for the sale of electricity to entities other than the end-user of power). The passage of the Energy Policy Act of 1992 (P.L. 102-486) served to further promote greater competition in the bulk power markets.[4] As a result, in many parts of the United States, the electric power industry began to transition from highly regulated, local monopoly companies which generated, transmitted, and distributed electricity to end-use customers, to a business in which power generation is competitive while the industry's transmission and distribution functions are still highly regulated. While the federal government regulates the electric power transmission function and wholesale power markets, regulation of the distribution function of the electric power business is still largely carried out by state government agencies.

Much of the infrastructure which serves the U.S. power grid is aging. The average age of power plants is now over 30 years; most of these facilities were originally designed to last 40 years.[5] Electric transmission and distribution system components are similarly aging, with power transformers averaging over 40 years of age,[6] and 70% of transmission lines being 25 years or older.[7] As components of the system are retired, they are replaced with newer components often linked to communications or automated systems.

With changes in federal law,[8] regulatory changes, and the aging of the electric power infrastructure as drivers, the grid is changing from a largely patchwork system built to serve the needs of individual electric utility companies to essentially a national interconnected system capable of accommodating massive transfers of electrical energy between regions of the United States. The modernization of the grid to accommodate today's power flows, serve reliability needs, and meet future projected uses is leading to the incorporation of information processing capabilities for power system controls and operations monitoring. The "Smart Grid" is the name given to the evolving electric power network as new information technology systems and

---

[1] EIA, *Glossary*, http://www.eia.gov/tools/glossary/index.cfm?id=B.

[2] EIA, *Glossary*, http://www.eia.gov/tools/glossary/index.cfm?id=B.

[3] As of 2007, there were 210 investor-owned electric utilities, 2,009 publicly-owned electric utilities, 883 consumer-owned rural electric cooperatives, and nine federal electric utilities. Energy Information Administration (EIA), *Electric Power Industry Overview 2007*, http://www.eia.doe.gov/electricity/page/prim2/toc2 html.

[4] The bulk power system makes it possible for utilities to engage in wholesale (sales for resale) electric power trade. U.S. Energy Information Administration, *Overview—Power Transactions & Interconnected Networks*, 2011, http://www.eia.gov/cneaf/electricity/page/prim2/chapter7 html.

[5] Massachusetts Institute of Technology, Retrofitting of Coal-Fired Power Plants for CO2 Emissions Reductions, March 23, 2009, http://web mit.edu/mitei/docs/reports/meeting-report.pdf.

[6] Thomas A. Prevost and David J. Woodcock, *Transformer Fleet Health and Risk Assessment*, Weidman Electrical Technology, IEEE PES Transformers Committee Tutorial, March 13, 2007, http://grouper.ieee.org/groups/transformers/info/S07/S07-TR_LifeExtension.pdf.

[7] K. Anderson, D. Furey, and K. Omar, *Frayed Wires: U.S. Transmission System Shows its Age*, Fitch Ratings, October 25, 2006.

[8] Key legislation include the Public Utility Regulatory Policies Act of 1978, the Energy Policy Acts of 1992 and 2005, and the Energy Independence and Security Act of 2007.

---

capabilities are incorporated. While these new components may add to the ability to control power flows and enhance the efficiency of grid operations, they also potentially increase the susceptibility of the grid to cyber (i.e., computer-related) attack since they are built around microprocessor devices whose basic functions are controlled by software programming and subject to manipulation over a network.

The information processing attributes which make the smarter grid attractive are the very same attributes which can increase the vulnerability of the electric power system and its critical infrastructure to a potentially devastating cyber attack. The potential of the Smart Grid to revolutionize the ways power is generated and used is great, but so too are the potential risks if not sufficiently addressed.

The Energy Independence and Security Act of 2007[9] (EISA) (P.L. 110-140) defined the attributes of a Smart Grid and plans for its development. The potential for a major disruption or widespread damage to the nation's power system from a large scale cyberattack has increased focus on the cybersecurity of the Smart Grid. While a nation-state might have the resources and capability to create widescale disruption of the U.S. grid (to create economic disorder or as part of a physical attack), terrorists or hackers are less likely to have the sophistication or resources necessary to inflict damage on a national scale. But the possibility of collaboration between terrorists and hackers could increase the capability of these groups to launch network-based cyberattacks against critical U.S. infrastructure.[10]

Among the issues for Congress is whether the existing requirements of current law adequately assure the cybersecurity and reliable operation of the U.S. electricity grid today (and the Smart Grid of tomorrow). This report will look at issues key to these determinations, discussing the scope and point of application of regulations, and where the overall responsibility rests for the cybersecurity of the grid.

Attributes of a Smart Grid

The U.S. Department of Energy (DOE) summarized its view of the potential of the Smart Grid by the year 2030 as:

> ... a fully automated power delivery network that monitors and controls every customer and node, ensuring a two-way flow of electricity and information between the power plant and the appliance, and all points in between. Its distributed intelligence, coupled with broadband communications and automated control systems, enables real-time market transactions and seamless interfaces among people, buildings, industrial plants, generation facilities, and the electric network.[11]

A "smarter" grid is gradually being introduced as upgrades to the systems and components of the power generation, transmission, and distribution infrastructure. Substation and distribution

---

[9] See Title XIII at 42 U.S.C. 17381 *et seq.*

[10] CRS Report R41674, *Terrorist Use of the Internet: Information Operations in Cyberspace*, by Catherine A. Theohary and John Rollins.

[11] United States Department of Energy, Office of Electric Transmission and Distribution, *"Grid 2030" A National Vision for Electricity's Second 100 Years*, July 2003, p. 27, http://www.oe.energy.gov/DocumentsandMedia/Electric_Vision_Document.pdf.

substations are being automated with superior switching capabilities to enhance current flows and control of the grid. Devices called "phasor measurement units" are also being added to substations to make time and location-specific measurements of transmission line voltage, current, and frequency (i.e., synchrophasor measurements made 30 times per second instead of data measured once every two to four seconds by current industrial control systems) providing better tools to improve power system reliability.[12] DOE's strategic plan targets the deployment of 1,000 phasor measurement units by 2013.[13]

Figure 2. One Conceptualization of the Smart Grid

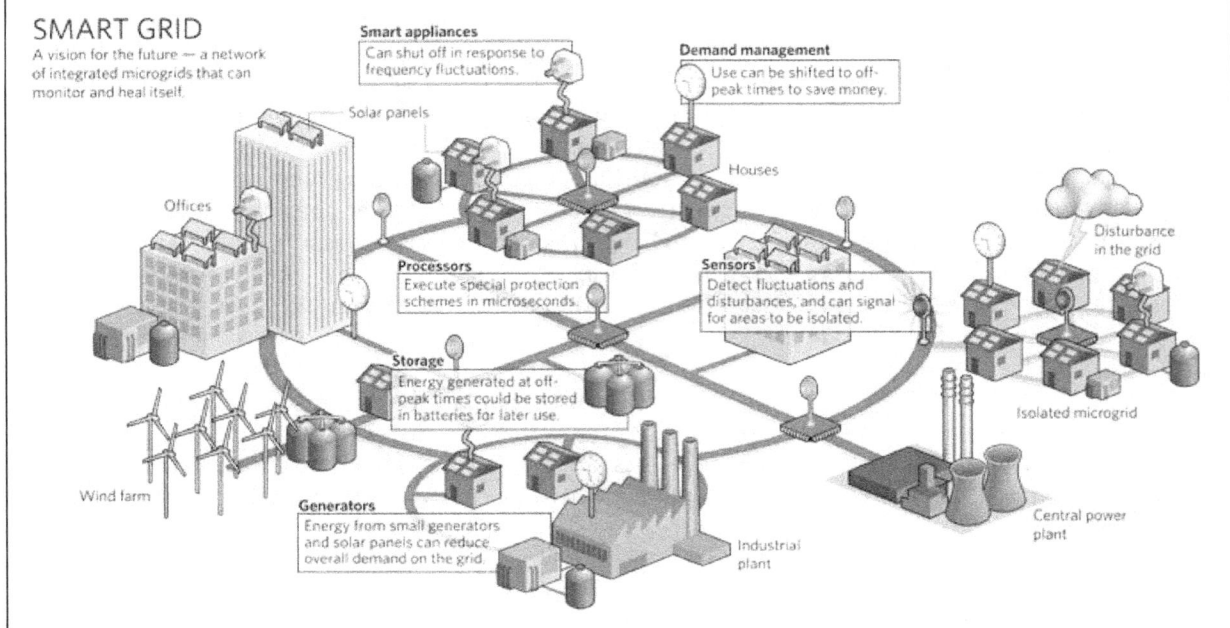

Source: Consumer Energy Report. See http://www.consumerenergyreport.com/wp-content/uploads/2010/04/smartgrid.jpg.

Advanced meters are being introduced in some utility markets which can offer customers the ability to leverage demand response[14] regimes and technologies, and potentially benefit from the interactive features of the Smart Grid by shifting their energy use to off-peak hours.

Expectations vary of what a Smart Grid could accomplish, and the estimated costs of a system rise with the increased scope and attributes of a system. Some see the Smart Grid as only an enhancement of today's existing transmission and distribution systems focused on improving the reliability and efficiency of the grid. Others see the Smart Grid of the future as an integrated system spanning the nation from coast to coast, able to seamlessly combine distributed resources

---

[12] Pacific Northwest National Laboratory, *North American SynchroPhasor Initiative*, May 2011, http://www.naspi.org/.

[13] U.S. Department of Energy, *Strategic Plan*, May 2011, http://www.energy.gov/news/documents/DOE_StrategicPlan.pdf.

[14] "Demand Response" allows retail customers to participate in electricity markets by giving them the ability to respond to prices as they change over time—either daily or hourly in most instances. See http://www.oe.energy.gov/demand.htm.

and central power stations across the three major interconnections[15] of the U.S. grid. Under such a vision, distributed and renewable energy resources could be efficiently integrated into the grid, with power from (for example) intermittent wind generation channeled by sensors and intelligent electronics from multiple widely dispersed sites to where power is needed anywhere on the grid. **Figure 2** shows a possible configuration of a Smart Grid system illustrating components of an interconnected, two-way intelligent network, and distributed and central station sources of power. The efficiency and economy of all grid operations could conceivably be optimized by similarly harnessing all power generation to take advantage of a wide range of generation and storage resources across the United States.

Defining Cybersecurity for the Smart Grid

A prolonged disruption of energy from the grid was described in a report for the Presidential Commission on Critical Infrastructure[16] as an event which would seriously affect every infrastructure, with the possibility of a cyberattack causing such damage considered as a possibility.

> The widespread and increasing use of Supervisory Control and Data Acquisition[17] (SCADA) systems for control of energy systems provides increasing ability to cause serious damage and disruption by cyber means. The exponential growth of information system networks that interconnect the business, administrative, and operational systems contributes to system vulnerability.[18]

EISA gave the National Institute of Standards and Technology (NIST) the role of coordinating the development of a framework to enable the development of the Smart Grid in a safe and secure manner, and NIST issued its first guidelines for cybersecurity of the Smart Grid in 2010. Because cybersecurity threats were perceived as "diverse and evolving," NIST advocated a defense-in-depth strategy with multiple levels of security because no single security measure could counter all types of threats.[19] The key to NIST's suggested approach is the determination of risk (i.e., the potential for an unwanted outcome resulting from internal or external factors, as determined from the likelihood of occurrence and the associated consequences) as quantified by the threat (e.g., event, actor or action with potential to do harm), the vulnerability (e.g., weakness in the system), and the consequences (e.g., physical impacts) to the system.[20]

---

[15] The Eastern, Western and Texas interconnections of the U.S. grid. See http://www.eia.doe.gov/cneaf/electricity/chg_stru_update/fig7 html.

[16] *Critical Foundations: Protecting America's Infrastructures*, The President's Commission on Critical Infrastructure Protection , October 1997, http://www fas.org/sgp/library/pccip.pdf. (CF)

[17] A system of remote control and telemetry used to monitor and control the transmission system. See http://www.eia.doe.gov/tools/glossary/index.cfm?id=S.

[18] CF, p. 12.

[19] The Smart Grid Interoperability Panel Cyber Security Working Group, *Introduction to NISTIR 7628*, National Institute of Standards and Technology, Guidelines for Smart Grid Cyber Security, September 2010, http://csrc nist.gov/publications/nistir/ir7628/introduction-to-nistir-7628.pdf. (NISTIR)

[20] NISTIR, p. 9.

Cybersecurity Vulnerabilities of the Smart Grid

A smarter grid is largely the result of the modernization of the grid. Most sectors of business and industry have gone from the analog age of knobs and dials to the digital age of sensors and electronic displays in the recent past, and that process is now reaching into the nation's electric power infrastructure. Part of the delay has been due to the long-lived nature of the capital assets which make up the industry. The power plants and other expensive components of the grid can function for many productive years if maintenance of the systems is kept up. However, much of the delay in modernization has been due to cost concerns, as many electric utilities seek to manage expenses by delaying replacement of aging systems as long as possible. Several of the better-known vulnerabilities of a smarter grid are discussed in the following paragraphs.

Control Systems

Industrial control (IC) systems are particularly vulnerable to cyberattack because of their intelligence and communications capabilities. IC systems perform a number of functions in the electrical grid, ranging from microprocessor-based control systems which control the actuation and operation of one or more devices, to more sophisticated industrial IC systems which can manage entire industrial processes or automated systems. SCADA systems are a well-known application of remote IC used to monitor and control electric transmission system components.

While cyber-intrusions into the U.S. grid have been reported in recent years,[21] no impairment or other damage has been publicly reported as a result of the attacks. By exploiting loopholes in cybersecurity, cyberattackers could breach the privacy of customers power usage data and access large numbers of meters, perhaps sending deliberately misleading information to the grid. This could potentially overload systems or cause grid operators to respond to false readings. However, concerns exist as to the potential damage that could result in the future from malware left behind by such intrusions or doorways created in systems which could be exploited.[22] The revelation of the complexities of the Stuxnet worm[23] and the alleged targeting of the control systems of a nuclear power plant in Iran[24] have raised additional concerns about the vulnerability of electric power systems worldwide.

---

[21] Siobhan Gordon, *Electricity Grid in U.S. Penetrated by Spies*, The Wall Street Journal, April 8, 2009, http://online.wsj.com/article/SB123914805204099085.html.

[22] Ibid.

[23] "[A worm is a]n independent computer program that reproduces by copying itself from one system to another across a network. Unlike computer viruses, worms do not require human involvement to propagate." See http://www.gao.gov/new.items/d09661t.pdf, p.6.

[24] "A successful attack by a software application such as the Stuxnet worm could result in manipulation of control system code to the point of inoperability or long-term damage. Should such an incident occur, recovery from the damage to the computer systems programmed to monitor and manage a facility and the physical equipment producing goods or services could be significantly delayed. Depending on the severity of the attack, the interconnected nature of the affected critical infrastructure facilities, and government preparation and response plans, entities and individuals relying on these facilities could be without life sustaining or comforting services for a long period of time. The resulting damage to the nation's critical infrastructure could threaten many aspects of life, including the government's ability to safeguard national security interests." CRS Report R41524, *The Stuxnet Computer Worm: Harbinger of an Emerging Warfare Capability*, by Paul K. Kerr, John Rollins, and Catherine A. Theohary.

The Stuxnet worm reportedly affected the logical decision making functions of the control systems of one particular type of manufacturing facility. Theoretically, Stuxnet-like malware could be adapted to impair other types of process or control systems in malicious or unpredictable ways. Malware modified in such ways could overload and damage targeted equipment and systems in critical infrastructure.[25] The Department of Homeland Security (DHS) conducted a simulated cyberattack on an electric generator control room and partially destroyed a large diesel-electric generator secured for the test as a demonstration of existing power system vulnerabilities.[26]

Connections Through Other Systems

Utilities have routinely accessed control systems either wirelessly or by telephone lines for many years. In fact, telephone lines often used to access corporate systems may even provide access to utility control systems. A recent GAO report highlighted vulnerabilities at the Tennessee Valley Authority, a large federal utility in the United States.

> ... the interconnections between TVA's control system networks and its corporate network increased the risk that security weaknesses, on the corporate network could affect control systems networks and we determined that the control systems were at increased risk of unauthorized modification or disruption by both internal and external threats.[27]

Communications and Internet Access

Grid devices capable of two-way communications are considered to be potential points of unauthorized system access, and can represent a potential cybersecurity vulnerability. While security protocols may exist to prevent unauthorized entry, wireless networks can be monitored and potentially hacked by cybercriminals. Smart meters are another example of new applications in which the security of data has been mentioned as a concern. At the heart of smart meters are semiconductor chips which allow data about energy use to be sent wirelessly to the electric distribution company, and which potentially allows the meter to control the flow of power to customers. The security of the encrypted information in the communications protocol used by many of these devices has been questioned in the past, and questions have been raised about the effectiveness of efforts to patch identified flaws. The primary consideration in the choice of wireless protocol by semiconductor providers seems to be cost of the system, a criteria which is not always compatible with cybersecurity goals for secure communications.[28] While the

---

[25] "The Stuxnet trojan/virus is the first publicly known 'worm' to target industrial control systems. The threat posed by Stuxnet has been portrayed as beyond anything seen before. Its goal was to sabotage a real-world industrial plant, not disrupt abstract IT systems. It was aimed at industrial control systems with the intention to reprogram PLCs [programmable logic controllers—devices used for control of processes] in a manner that would sabotage the plant, hiding the changes from programmers or users. Stuxnet has highlighted the potential to directly attack industrial control systems used in critical national infrastructure, including energy, water, and transport sectors." Richard Piggin, *Control Network Security Lessons from Stuxnet*, Consulting-Specifying Engineer, February 3, 2011, http://m.csemag.com/index.php?id=2832&tx_ttnews%5Btt_news%5D=42715&cHash=42da992b88.

[26] Military Photos.net, *AURORA Test Validated Fears of Dept. of Homeland Security*, October 1, 2007, http://www.militaryphotos.net/forums/showthread.php?121081-AURORA-test-validated-fears-of-Dept.-of-Homeland-Security.

[27] U.S. Government Accountability Office, *INFORMATION SECURITY Cyber Threats and Vulnerabilities Place Federal Systems at Risk*, GAO-09-661T, May 5, 2009, p. 12, http://www.gao.gov/new.items/d09661t.pdf.

[28] Jeffrey Carr, "Ember Needs a Wake-Up Call from the CIA," *Forbes*, January 31, 2011, http://blogs.forbes.com/ (continued...)

---

developing Smart Grid is likely to use today's internet and wireless communications systems for many years to come, security concerns and data usage requirements may move the system to dedicated communications and information channels serving uniquely Smart Grid uses.

Potential access to SCADA systems via the Internet has often been cited as a key vulnerability for electric power systems. Hackers have used the Internet to launch denial of service,[29] phishing,[30] and various other forms of cyberattack. The effective recording, processing, and exchanging of data is becoming increasingly critical to the reliability of the power system,[31] and deliberately introduced misinformation can be damaging. Internet-linked communications systems may be important to today's interconnected grid, but the Internet also provides a ready path to cyberattack from any corner of the world wide web.

Combined Cyber- and Physical Attacks

The vulnerability of key components of the grid to a physical attack has been long known, but a coordinated and sustained physical and/or cyberattack[32] could be problematic. After a cyberattack, restored systems may be repaired and protected against known vulnerabilities, but a coordinated cyberattack over a short time period targeting different Smart Grid systems could slow recovery. The same would hold true for repeated physical attacks, or combined cyber- and physical attacks on key grid components. Under such circumstances, the resources of emergency programs in place to replace important grid systems and components (such as the Edison Electric Institute's "Spare Transformer Equipment Program"[33]) may not be adequate to provide enough replacement parts to fully restore reliable grid operations in a timely manner.

Supply Chain

The components of smarter grid devices present another potential vulnerability concern. Most of the smart meter, sensor, and other equipment makers are international companies who obtain their components from international sources. Taiwan, Singapore, China, and South Korea are among the largest overseas manufacturers of semiconductors and microprocessors for smart devices. The reliable operation of semiconductor and microprocessor-based devices is based on the low-level firmware[34] controlling the device's basic functions. Firmware in the form of fixed machine-

---

(...continued)
jeffreycarr/2011/01/31/ember-needs-a-wake-up-call-from-the-cia/.

[29] A method of attack that denies system access to legitimate users without actually having to compromise the targeted system. From a single source, the attack overwhelms the target computers with messages and blocks legitimate traffic. It can prevent one system from being able to exchange data with other systems or prevent the system from using the Internet. See http://www.gao.gov/new.items/d09661t.pdf, p.5.

[30] A high-tech scam that frequently uses spam or pop-up messages to deceive people into disclosing sensitive information. Internet scammers use e-mail bait to "phish" for passwords and financial information from the sea of internet users. See http://www.gao.gov/new.items/d09661t.pdf, p. 6.

[31] NISTIR. Page 7.

[32] James St. Pierre, *Smart Grid Interoperability Panel Cyber Security Working Group*, National Institute of Standards and Technology, Presentation at National Electricity Forum, Washington, DC, February 16-17, 2011, p. 10, http://www.nationalelectricityforum.org/pdfs/NationalElectricityForum_StPierre_2011Feb08.pdf.

[33] Edison Electric Institute, *Spare Transformers*, 2011, http://www.eei.org/ourissues/ElectricityTransmission/Pages/SpareTransformers.aspx.

[34] Software that is embedded in a hardware device that allows reading and executing the software, but does not allow modification, e.g., writing or deleting data by an end user. See http://www.its.bldrdoc.gov/fs-1037/dir-015/_2236 htm.

---

language binary code is found in almost all the electronic devices making up smarter grid products such as programmable controllers and programmable logic arrays. If a hacker or cybercriminal gained access to such devices (especially during the manufacturing process), a section of code could be covertly inserted in the device and activated in such a way as to impair its functioning in a reliable manner. Some might suggest random or statistically based testing of the firmware in smarter grid devices. But the impairment would not need to be placed in all such devices coming off an assembly line. If a large enough sample was impaired, the effect might be enough to cast doubt on the reliability of a whole class of such devices.

Geomagnetic Impairment

An electromagnetic pulse (EMP) is a large burst of electromagnetic radiation resulting from the detonation of a nuclear weapon or from other means. EMPs can cause voltage and current surges which can severely damage electrical equipment and systems. A high-altitude nuclear explosion could cause an EMP which could severely impair an electric power system not shielded from the effects of an EMP.

However, deliberate, large-scale, man-made attacks are not the only potential threat which could take down a substantial portion of the electric grid. Radiation or charged particles ejected into space weather from solar flare eruptions could cause geomagnetic storms which could interfere with telecommunications networks or damage orbiting satellites. Periodically, these eruptions from the sun are powerful enough to disrupt the operations of electric power systems. Solar flares occur in cycles of almost 11 years. [35] Occasionally, severe space weather results in a huge eruption of particles which can be particularly disruptive to electric power systems, and induce ground currents powerful enough to actually melt the copper windings of electric power transformers. The last major solar flare eruption in 1989 caused blackouts across the Canadian province of Quebec for nine hours. But even greater storms can occur perhaps every 100 or more years. The first major eruption of this size was observed in 1859. It destroyed much of the world's telegraph infrastructure of the time. Another event observed in 1921 demonstrates that although these events are rare, they are likely to occur again and could have tremendous societal and economic impacts for the United States:

> … the occurrence today of an event like the 1921 storm would result in large-scale blackouts affecting more than 130 million people and would expose more than 350 transformers to the risk of permanent damage. [36]

It could take weeks or months to replace most of the damaged transformers. Some of the larger units could take years to replace due to the fact there are no U.S. power transformer manufacturers, [37] and a multi-year backlog exists for the larger units.

---

[35] Committee on the Societal and Economic Impacts of Severe Space Weather Events, National Research Council, *Severe Space Weather Events—Understanding Societal and Economic Impacts: A Workshop Report*, National Academies, May 22-23, 2008, http://books.nap.edu/catalog.php?record_id=12507.

[36] Ibid.

[37] Yousaf M. Butt, "The EMP Threat: Fact, Fiction, and Response," *Space Review*, February 1, 2010, http://www.thespacereview.com/article/1553/2.

Current Cybersecurity Policy for the Smart Grid

A smarter grid is increasing reliance on automated systems to manage energy sources, power control devices, system information, and power flows. Automation will allow information from smarter processors and sensors to be processed at much faster rates, giving power system operators more accurate and timely information, and giving customers greater input into their own power use. But, the possibility that such systems could be highjacked in such a way as to bring down the grid regionally or even nationally, and cause long-term damage to critical systems and components, is giving Congress reason to consider the cybersecurity of the electric power infrastructure.

The passage of the Homeland Security Act of 2002 (P.L. 107-296) (HSA) established the Department of Homeland Security. HSA increased penalties for certain computer-based crimes, and in addition to improving on the earlier Computer Fraud and Abuse Act of 1986,[38] made critical infrastructure protection a key mission of DHS.

Federal efforts to enhance the cybersecurity of the electrical grid were reemphasized with the recognition of cybersecurity as a critical issue for electric utilities in developing the Smart Grid. The Energy Independence and Security Act (EISA) of 2007 (P.L. 110-140) thus added requirements for "a reliable and secure electricity infrastructure" with regard to Smart Grid development. EISA directed NIST to develop a framework for protocols and standards for the Smart Grid to achieve "interoperability"[39] of devices and systems. The American Recovery and Reinvestment Act of 2009 (P.L. 111-5) provided NIST with funds to proceed with this mandate.

Status of Regulatory Implementation

NIST issued a report, "NIST Framework and Roadmap for Smart Grid Interoperability Standards" (NIST SP 1108, January 2010), listing 75 existing standards which are likely to be applicable for an interoperable Smart Grid, and identified 15 high-priority gaps and harmonization issues. NIST also issued a "Smart Grid Cybersecurity Strategy and Requirements" report (NISTIR 7628, September 2010) assessing requirements to ensure the security and reliability of a modernized grid. This report also classified Smart Grid interfaces according to potential impacts that could result from compromise of these systems.

The Federal Energy Regulatory Commission (FERC or the Commission) received primary responsibility for the reliability of the bulk power[40] system from the Energy Policy Act of 2005 (EPACT05) (P.L. 109-58). EPACT05 also gave FERC the authority to commission an "Electric Reliability Organization" (ERO) to establish and enforce reliability standards. FERC subsequently designated the North American Electric Reliability Corporation (NERC) as the ERO. Compliance with reliability standards for electric utilities thus changed from a voluntary,

---

[38] 18 U.S.C. § 1030.

[39] Interoperability can be defined as the capability of two or more networks, systems, devices, applications, or components to share and readily use information securely and effectively with little or no inconvenience to the user. GridWise Architecture Council, *Interoperability Path Forward Whitepaper*, November 30, 2005, http://www.gridwiseac.org/pdfs/interoperability_path_whitepaper_v1_0.pdf.

[40] The electrical generation resources, transmission lines, interconnections with neighboring systems, and associated equipment, generally operated at voltages of 100 kV or higher. http://www.nerc.com/files/Glossary_2009April20.pdf.

---

peer-driven undertaking to a mandatory function. While NERC is responsible for standards for the bulk power system in the United States, it is also seeking recognition by applicable governmental authorities in Canada and Mexico to establish and coordinate reliability standards for the bulk power systems of these respective countries.[41] NERC is also responsible for standards for critical infrastructure protection (CIP) which focus on planning and procedures for the physical security of the grid. NERC has delegated much of the daily process of maintaining reliability of the grid to regional entities via delegation agreements which are subject to FERC approval. Compliance and enforcement with NERC standards is therefore largely a responsibility of these regional entities, which are mostly responsible for imposing penalties for violation of reliability standards.[42] NERC's CIP standards essentially approach cybersecurity as an extension of reliability, and address nine areas including *Sabotage Reporting*, *Critical Cyber Asset Identification*, and *Electronic Security Perimeters*, and *Recovery Plans for Critical Cyber Assets*.[43] These standards identify what utilities must do to protect "cyber assets"[44] seen as critical to the reliability of the bulk power[45] system.

EISA directed FERC to work with NIST in developing Smart Grid interoperability standards, and required FERC to institute a formal rulemaking process to adopt interoperability (including cybersecurity) standards when FERC was satisfied that a consensus on defining the standards had been reached. NIST advised FERC in October 2010 that it had identified five "foundational" sets of standards[46] which may allow FERC to go forward with instituting rulemaking proceedings to adopt standards to ensure Smart Grid functionality, interoperability, and cybersecurity. The standards would be updated as Smart Grid requirements and technologies evolve.

FERC held a technical conference in January 2011 to determine if there was "sufficient consensus" that the five sets of standards proposed by NIST were adequate for standards and protocols to be adopted. The comments of conference participants showed that a consensus on the standards had not in fact been reached with several participants stating that they were unsure of what would constitute a consensus, and questioning whether such standards would then automatically become "mandatory and enforceable." FERC issued a supplemental notice in February 2011 (requesting all comments by April 2011) to aid the Commission's determination as to whether a consensus exists on the proposed NIST interoperability standards. Additional questions were asked in the notice to solicit opinions on related topics including the NIST process for determining the readiness of a standard with regards to interoperability and cybersecurity, whether making standards enforceable would achieve interoperability goals, how testing and

---

[41] North American Electric Reliability Corporation, *Rules of Procedure*, March 21, 2008, http://www.nerc.com/files/NERC_Rules_of_Procedure_EFFECTIVE_20080321.pdf.

[42] The maximum civil penalty which can be assessed for violation of reliability standards is $1 million per day. *Revised Policy Statement on Penalty Guidelines*, 132 FERC ¶ 61,216, issued September 17, 2010.

[43] North American Electric Reliability Corporation, *Reliability Standards for the Bulk Electric Systems of North America*, April 20, 2010, http://www.nerc.com/files/Reliability_Standards_Complete_Set.pdf.

[44] Programmable electronic devices and communication networks including hardware, software, and data. http://www.nerc.com/files/Glossary_2009April20.pdf.

[45] In FERC Order No. 743, the North American Electric Reliability Corporation was directed to revise its definition of the term "bulk electric system" to ensure that the definition encompasses all facilities necessary for operating an interconnected electric transmission network. The revision will be made in accordance with NERC's Reliability Standards development process. See http://www.ferc.gov/whats-new/comm-meet/2010/111810/E-2.pdf.

[46] The standards produced by the International Electrotechnical Commission (IEC) focus on the informational models and procedures necessary to promote the reliable and efficient operation of the Smart Grid. Standard IEC 62351 specifically addresses the cyber security of communications protocols.

certification of cybersecurity requirements could be incorporated into the standards process, and whether the Commission should consider different criteria for evaluating interoperability and functionality (and the extent to which cybersecurity is an element of each).[47]

Assessment of Cybersecurity Progress by Government Accountability Office

Congress asked the U.S. Government Accountability Office (GAO) to assess progress by NIST and FERC on Smart Grid cybersecurity guidelines and standards. GAO issued a report with its findings in January 2011.[48] GAO found that NIST has largely addressed "key cybersecurity elements" such as the cybersecurity risks of Smart Grid systems and had identified security controls essential to such systems. GAO also found that NIST had not addressed the risks of attacks on Smart Grid systems using both cyber- and physical means. GAO recommended that NIST finalize its plan and schedule for updating its cybersecurity guidelines to include these elements.

GAO also pointed out that while EISA had given FERC authority to adopt Smart Grid standards, it did not give FERC specific enforcement authority over implementation of standards. GAO recognized that a regulatory divide exists between federal, state, and local entities on various aspects of Smart Grid interoperability and cybersecurity. As such, GAO states that such standards will remain voluntary unless regulators use other authorities to enforce standards compliance. GAO recommended that FERC develop a coordinated approach (with other regulatory jurisdictions) to monitor voluntary standards and address any gaps in compliance.

FERC and NIST agreed with GAO's recommendations.[49] However, FERC Chairman Wellinghoff stated that while a coordinated approach would be pursued, FERC may lack the authority to address any gaps in compliance, and that this being the case, Congress may want to consider the matter further. Furthermore, in addressing GAO's comments, the Chairman broached the question of whether other-than-voluntary compliance with Smart Grid standards by "relevant manufacturers and utilities" is what Congress intended in EISA.[50]

Meanwhile, NIST has communicated to FERC its own concerns that under the existing process, it could take years for the Commission to adopt rules on the many individual standards needed to achieve interoperability of the Smart Grid while recognizing that many "customized" upgrades to the grid continue to be installed. NIST suggested that in the absence of formal standards, FERC could request "interoperability roadmaps" from utilities to determine if they addressed interoperability based on the NIST framework in the utilities' grid modernization efforts.[51]

---

[47] Federal Energy Regulatory Commission, *Smart Grid Interoperability Standards—Supplemental Notice Requesting Comments*, February 16, 2011, http://www.ferc.gov/EventCalendar/Files/20110228084004-supplemental-notice.pdf.

[48] U.S. Government Accountability Office, *Electricity Grid Modernization: Progress Being Made on Cybersecurity Guidelines, but Key Challenges Remain to be Addressed*, GAO-11-117, January 12, 2011, http://www.gao.gov/products/GAO-11-117.

[49] Ibid, p. 27.

[50] Federal Energy Regulatory Commission, Letter from FERC Chairman Wellinghoff to David A. Powner, Director, Information Technology Management Issues for the United States Government Accountability Office, December 23, 2010, http://www.ferc.gov/industries/electric/indus-act/smart-grid/wellinghoff-response-GAO.pdf.

[51] Letter from G. Arnold, NIST to FERC Chairman J. Wellinghoff, dated April 7, 2011. See http://www.nist.gov/smartgrid/upload/FERC_Letter1.pdf.

Assessment by DOE's Inspector General of FERC's Monitoring of Grid Cybersecurity

The DOE Inspector General released an audit report[52] in January 2011 of FERC's monitoring of grid cybersecurity, with regard to the Commission's responsibilities under EPACT05. The report found that CIP cybersecurity standards developed "did not include a number of security controls commonly recommended for government and industry systems," and criticized FERC's oversight of the process for developing these standards, citing a need for FERC to use its existing authority to ensure timely standards development to address emerging security threats. The report also said that FERC's implementation approach and schedule for CIP standards did not adequately consider risks to information systems, since FERC was focusing on documentation of controls rather than implementation of controls. FERC was advised to revise its focus to ensure that controls to address higher threat risks are given priority. The report noted that these problems existed, in part, because the Commission had "only limited authority" to ensure cybersecurity over the bulk electric system, and could not implement its own reliability standards or issue alerts. However, the report went on to conclude that even "when such authority did exist," FERC did not always act "to ensure that cybersecurity standards were adequate."

FERC Chairman Wellinghoff mostly concurred with the report's recommendations[53] while noting that "the current statutory framework is adequate for addressing emerging cybersecurity threats through mandatory standards." The Chairman stated that FERC will make every effort "to approve CIP standards as soon as possible after they are developed by NERC."[54]

Policy Concerns

Self-determination is a key part of the CIP reliability process. Utilities are allowed to self-identify what they see as "critical assets"[55] under NERC regulations. While compliance with CIP standards became mandatory in 2010, FERC mandated modifications to the criteria defining critical assets for reliability purposes. Only "critical cyber-assets" (i.e., as essential to the reliable operation of critical assets) are subject to CIP standards. FERC directed NERC to revise the standards so that some oversight of the identification process for critical cyber-assets was provided, but any revision is again subject to stakeholder approval. Under current law, FERC cannot issue its own reliability standards.

While reliability standards are mandatory, the ERO process for developing regulations is somewhat unusual in that the regulations are essentially being established by the entities who are being regulated.[56] This can potentially be an issue when cost of compliance is a concern, and

---

[52] U.S. Department of Energy, Office of Inspector General, *Audit Report, Federal Energy Regulatory Commission's Monitoring of Power Grid Cyber Security*, January 2011, http://www.ig.energy.gov/documents/IG-0846.pdf. (DOEIG).

[53] DOEIG, pages 11-12.

[54] DOEIG, pages 21-22.

[55] Defined by NERC as "facilities, systems, and equipment which, if destroyed, degraded, or otherwise rendered unavailable, would affect the reliability or operability of the bulk electric system." See http://www.nerc.com/files/Glossary_of_Terms_2011Mar15.pdf.

[56] NERC works with eight regional entities to improve the reliability of the bulk power system. The members of the regional entities come from all segments of the electric industry: investor-owned utilities; federal power agencies; rural electric cooperatives; state, municipal and provincial utilities; independent power producers; power marketers; and end-use customers. These entities account for virtually all the electricity supplied in the United States, Canada, and a (continued...)

---

acceptable standards may conceivably result from the option with the lowest costs. While FERC ultimately has approval authority over the regulations NERC submits and can remand such regulations it judges as not satisfying requirements, any such revisions are ultimately subject to NERC stakeholder approval. NERC standards could therefore be seen as a minimum threshold for compliance, as some utilities may choose to go beyond what is minimally required. But since utility systems are interconnected in many ways, the system with the least protected network potentially provides the weakest point of access.

Other Issues in Federal Smart Grid Cybersecurity Policy

Legacy Systems

Legacy devices and systems (such as many SCADA and substation automation systems) may represent as much of a vulnerability to cybersecurity as new Smart Grid components. They were not designed with cybersecurity in mind, and are often interconnected either via the Internet or by other, sometimes "unsecured" avenues. DOE describes the legacy system communications issue as follows:

> The legacy communication methods that now support grid operations also provide potential cyber attack paths. Many cyber vulnerabilities have been identified by cyber security assessments of SCADA systems. Power grid substation automation and security have also recently been evaluated. The level of automation in substations is increasing, which can lead to more cyber security issues. The cyber security issues identified during the assessments and evaluations need to be resolved, but the known issues should not be construed as a complete assessment of the current power grid security posture.[57]

Some legacy grid devices are being retrofitted with communications capabilities to allow them functionality in the smarter grid, or permit easier maintenance, potentially introducing grid vulnerabilities which may not have existed before. NIST has suggested the establishment of "Priority Actions Plans" to resolve interoperability issues between legacy equipment and Smart Grid systems as these are installed.[58]

FERC specifically rejected proposals by commenters for additional interoperability standards (at this time) addressing existing resources or equipment and cost-effective integration of legacy equipment, and interfaces between utilities.[59] Replacement of these systems is recognized by

---

(...continued)

portion of Baja California Norte, Mexico. See http://www.nerc.com/page.php?cid=1%7C9%7C119.

[57] U.S. Department of Energy Office of Electricity Delivery and Energy Reliability, *Study of Security Attributes of Smart Grid Systems—Current Cyber Security Issues*, INL/EXT-09-15500, April 2009, http://www.inl.gov/scada/publications/d/securing_the_smart_grid_current_issues.pdf.

[58] National Institute of Standards and Technology, *NIST Framework and Roadmap for Smart Grid Interoperability Standards, Release 1.0*, NIST Special Publication 1108, January 2010, http://www.nist.gov/public_affairs/releases/upload/smartgrid_interoperability_final.pdf.

[59] On July 16, 2009, the Commission issued a Smart Grid Policy Statement in which, among other things, the Commission explained its view that EISA does not make any Smart Grid standards mandatory and does not give the Commission authority to make or enforce any such standards. The Commission clarified that, under current law, its (continued...)

FERC as a possible option for utilities to apply for recovery of the "stranded costs" of legacy systems replaced by Smart Grid investments.[60]

Leadership of Federal Authority for Smart Grid Cybersecurity

The issue of which, or whether, a single federal agency should have ultimate authority over Smart Grid cybersecurity remains largely unresolved. DHS, DOE, and FERC have all either stated claims or been mentioned as candidates for overall leadership of the issue based upon implications to national security, energy policy and technology leadership, or industry understanding and organizational mission, but the current missions of these agencies is only the starting point for a discussion. Since Smart Grid devices are being installed beyond the federally regulated power grid, the system could potentially face intrusions from cyberattacks initiated on less-protected distribution systems. Leadership of Smart Grid and cybersecurity issues may require the ability to communicate issues and push solutions in forums beyond federal jurisdictions if the goal is to protect against cyber-threats to the grid for the entire United States.

DHS's mission to protect national security against cyber-threats currently centers on "civilian government systems" and DHS works with industry to "secure critical infrastructure and information systems." DHS is focused on analyzing cyber-threats and reducing vulnerabilities, and distributing information on potential cyberattacks to ensure the safety of cybersystems.[61] DHS will distribute warnings of cyber-threats to other federal agencies, state and local governments and to industry.

DOE has the technical and research capabilities of the national laboratories to draw upon with regard to cybersecurity and the Smart Grid, as well as its own internal policy offices which deal with an array of electricity system issues. DOE has worked with electric utilities to understand the cyber-vulnerabilities of the grid, and has tasked the national laboratories with helping to develop technologies and software patches to identify problems and harden legacy control systems against potential cyber-intrusions.

FERC is an independent, self-funded regulatory agency within DOE, with statutory authority over major aspects of the wholesale electric, natural gas, hydroelectric, and oil pipeline industries.[62] As such, FERC's responsibility for the reliability of the grid and related ratemaking authority allow the Commission to discover issues and authorize utilities to recover the jurisdictional portion of costs related to grid critical infrastructure protection upgrades. FERC recognizes that EISA does

---

(...continued)

authority, if any, to make Smart Grid standards mandatory [or allow recovery in rates] derives from the Federal Power Act. *Smart Grid Policy*, 128 FERC ¶ 61,060, issued July 16, 2009. See http://www.ferc.gov/whats-new/comm-meet/ 2009/071609/E-3.pdf. (FERCSGP)

[60] The Commission also proposed to permit applicants to seek recovery of the otherwise stranded costs of legacy systems that are to be replaced by smart grid equipment. The Commission stated that an appropriate plan for the staged deployment of smart grid equipment, which could include appropriate upgrades to legacy systems where technically feasible and cost-effective, could help minimize the stranding of unamortized costs of legacy systems. The Commission therefore proposed that any request to recover stranded legacy system costs must demonstrate that such a migration plan has been developed. FERCSGP. Page 82.

[61] Department of Homeland Security, *Safeguard and Secure Cyberspace*, http://www.dhs.gov/xabout/ gc_1240609042614.shtm.

[62] Federal Energy Regulatory Commission, *FY 2010 Performance and Accountability Report*, November 2010, http://www.ferc.gov/about/strat-docs/2010-audit.pdf.

not make Smart Grid standards mandatory, nor does EISA give it authority to make or enforce such standards.[63] FERC has jurisdiction over the bulk power system, but this currently excludes authority over the nation's electric distribution systems where much of the smarter grid will be deployed. The Commission appears to view its reliability mandate under EISA as giving it the authority to adopt Smart Grid standards which will be applicable to all electric power facilities and devices with Smart Grid features, including those at the distribution level. FERC further ties cybersecurity to reliability by proposing a "harmonization" of each Smart Grid protocol and reliability standard developed. [64]

Cost Challenges of Maintaining a Cyber-Secure Smart Grid

Cybersecurity threats present a constantly moving and growing need for mitigation activities. As new devices and systems are being developed for the Smart Grid, so too is the array of infrastructure elements which must potentially be protected. This is a key concern for utilities, as the resources which may have to be applied to cybersecurity concerns could likewise spiral upward in growth and costs. Utilities may understand how a smarter grid can enhance their efficiency and reliability, and the need for cybersecurity safeguards. Commercial and industrial customers may also see potential benefits in Smart Grid-enabled programs (such as demand response), and it is likely they will fund a significant portion of smarter grid improvements through rates. But at present very few consumers at the residential level seem to understand the potential of the Smart Grid, or have reason to believe it can do anything for them except increase rates.[65] One recent study expects cybersecurity spending to represent approximately 15% of total Smart Grid capital investment between 2010 and 2015 (with total investment estimated to be $1.5 billion in North America).[66]

Smart Grid enhancements across the United States may vary by utility, state, region, and regulatory jurisdiction. Recovery of costs may present a major challenge especially to distribution utilities and state commissions charged with overseeing utility costs. When faced with such decisions, the perception of the potential risks to the utility's local system will likely bear on what costs the utility's ratepayers should pay. EISA requires states only to consider recovery of costs related to Smart Grid systems. FERC has jurisdiction over the bulk power grid, i.e., transmission and wholesale rates in interstate commerce. FERC cannot compel entities involved in distribution to comply with its regulations. Since distribution utilities are regulated by state or local public utility commissions, Smart Grid investments will likely require approval by these jurisdictions. The issue of whether Smart Grid standards for interoperability should be voluntary or mandatory for these jurisdictions remains unresolved.

---

[63] See footnote 58.

[64] FERCSGP, p. 27.

[65] M. D. Garratt, *Distributech Highlights Challenge of SmartGrid: What's in it for Consumers?*, CleanMakesGreen.com, February 7, 2011, http://cleanmakesgreen.com/2011/02/07/distributech-highlights-challenge-of-smartgrid-what%E2%80%99s-in-it-for-consumers/.

[66] Business Wire, *Smart Grid Cyber Security Market to Reach $3.7 Billion by 2015, According to Pike Research*, Smart Grid Cyber Security, June 23, 2010, http://www.businesswire.com/portal/site/home/permalink/?ndmViewId=news_view&newsId=20100623005613&newsLang=en.

Privacy and Data Security

The sharing of information in applications used by the smarter grid has raised questions on the safety of that information. Security of customer information in wireless applications, and how personal data characteristics (such as customer usage information) can be protected are issues often mentioned in discussions of the Smart Grid and cybersecurity. Encryption of data (with limited decryption for data checking), and aggregation of data at high levels to mask individual usership have been mentioned as ways to protect the identity of individual customers. Limiting the amount of data to just information needed for billing purposes has been suggested as a remedy to the potential for misuse of data.[67] Real-time monitoring of these networks may alert system operators to suspicious activities. But even these methods might not be enough to guard against a sophisticated intruder if data security is taken for granted. The development of Smart Grid standards for electric utilities and their partners governing the collection and use of customer data may be a possible next step.

If customers participate in demand-side management programs, then customer usage data can provide a wealth of information for a variety of programs for interruptible loads or time-of-use rates. But customer-specific data stored in home area networks (HANs), or customer-specific data communicated between the HAN and distribution utility (or load aggregator) must be secure to protect the privacy of information. The advent of electric vehicles may offer another potential payload of data on customer movement and habits, if data collected or stored is not restricted to electricity consumption for billing purposes.

The National Regulatory Research Institute recommended in a recent report[68] that public utility commissions should define the information which utilities will collect, determining with whom and for what purpose it should be shared, and assess the need for protecting the data. While allowing states to develop their own policies may be accomplished more quickly, the report also advocates for a national approach to Smart Grid privacy issues.

DOE has worked with electric utilities and the Electric Power Research Institute (EPRI) to develop profiles for Smart Grid products to address concerns about data privacy. These profiles are meant to provide guidance on how to build cybersecurity into Smart Grid applications under development, so that they can be more securely integrated into the Smart Grid.[69]

Government-Industry Coordination on Threats

In 2010, the Edison Electric Institute (EEI) issued its own "Principles for Cyber Security and Critical Infrastructure Protection"[70] to discuss development of a framework for addressing

---

[67] Mathew J. Schwartz, *California Proposes Smart Grid Data Privacy Standards*, Information Week, May 18, 2011, http://mobile.informationweek.com/10247/show/8d96dc971db09af9557e4ad59b4708df&t= f6de813a074007af2879af82d46659ef.

[68] Sherry Lichtenberg, *Smart Grid Data: Must There Be Conflict Between Energy Management and Consumer Privacy?*, National Regulatory Research Institute, December 2010, http://www.nrri.org/pubs/telecommunications/ NRRI_smart_grid_privacy_dec10-17.pdf.

[69] Patricia Hoffman, *Statement Before the U.S. Senate Committee on Energy and Natural Resources*, Office of Electricity Delivery and Energy Reliability - U.S. Department of Energy, Cybersecurity of the bulk-power system and electric infrastructure, May 5, 2011, p. 5, http://energy.senate.gov/public/_files/HoffmanTestimony050511.pdf.

[70] See http://www.eei.org/ourissues/ElectricityTransmission/Documents/cyber_security_principles.pdf.

cybersecurity threats. EEI, the trade association of U.S. shareholder-owned electric utilities, suggested a coordinated effort of government, industry, and suppliers of critical grid systems and components was necessary to protect the grid from cyberattacks as a "shared responsibility." EEI believes that the sharing of intelligence on evolving threats and a clear plan of action on imminent threats is key to this arrangement. EEI also expects that such a policy would help protect national security and the public welfare, and aid in the prioritization of assets which need enhanced security. EEI expects that such a partnership could "utilize all stakeholder's expertise," allowing owners and operators of critical infrastructure to propose mitigation strategies that will avoid significant adverse consequences to utility operation or assets.

Other Collaborative Cybersecurity Initiatives

There are a number of collaborative efforts involving private sector, academia, national laboratories, consumer groups, and others looking at cybersecurity and Smart Grid issues. Federal agencies are also working together to ensure communication and share resources on these issues, and helping to fund industry cybersecurity initiatives.[71] Two of the major DOE-led initiatives are discussed below.

DOE is home to the Federal Smart Grid Task Force (FSGTF) established under EISA to "ensure awareness, coordination, and integration of the diverse activities of DOE's Office of Electricity Delivery and Energy Reliability (OE) and elsewhere in the federal government related to Smart Grid technologies, practices, and services."[72] FERC, the Department of Commerce, the Environmental Protection Agency, the Department of Agriculture, and the Department of Defense are also members of the FSGTF.

DOE also funds (with OE leading DOE's participation) the "Trustworthy Cyber Infrastructure for the Power Grid" (TCIPG) initiative, working with DHS and industry.[73] TCIPG is led by the academic sector as a public-private research partnership, supporting the development of resilient and secure Smart Grid systems, leveraging research previously funded by the National Science Foundation:

> TCIPG's research plan is focused on securing the low-level devices, communications, and data systems that make up the power grid, to ensure trustworthy operation during normal conditions, cyber-attacks, and/or power emergencies. At the device level, new key functionality is being designed in hardware in order to detect attacks and failures and to restore proper system operation. Likewise, virtual machine technology is being developed and adapted for advanced power meters in order to permit new power use scenarios while preserving privacy. At the protocol level, new techniques are being developed to detect, react to, and recover from cyber attacks that occur while preserving integrity, availability, and real-time requirements.

---

[71] Electric Light & Power.com, *DOE Picks EPRI Collaborative to Lead Cybersecurity Project*, December 27, 2010, http://www.elp.com/index/display/article-display/6433556709/articles/electric-light-power/policy-and_regulation/2010/09/DOE_picks_EPRI_collaborative_to_lead_cybersecurity_project_.html.

[72] U.S. Department of Energy, *Federal Smart Grid Task Force*, http://www.oe.energy.gov/smartgrid_taskforce.htm.

[73] Trustworthy Cyber Infrastructure for the Power Grid, *About TCIPG*, 2011, http://tcipg.org/about-tcipg-trustworthy-cyber-infrastructure-power-grid.

Participating in TCIPG are the University of Illinois at Urbana-Champaign, Dartmouth College, Cornell University, the University of California at Davis, and Washington State University. Current TCIPG projects are focused on developing "trustworthy cyber infrastructure and technologies" for active demand management and wide-area monitoring and control, response to and managing cyber events, and risk/security assessments.

Current Legislation

Several bills introduced in the 112th Congress addressing the cybersecurity of the Smart Grid are summarized below.

Senate

The Cyber Security and American Cyber Competitiveness Act of 2011[74] (S. 21) would secure the United States against cyberattack and protect sensitive information and the identities of U.S. citizens and business. The bill focuses on the increasing dependence of the United States on information technology, and highlights a growing need for public awareness and preparedness of cyber-threats.

The Cybersecurity and Internet Freedom Act of 2011[75] (S. 413) is intended to enhance the "security and resiliency of the cyber and communications infrastructure" of the United States. Among its provisions, the bill would establish within DHS a National Center for Cybersecurity and Communications (NCCC) to protect the federal and national information infrastructure. The duties of the NCCC Director would include the identification and evaluation of cyber-risks to critical infrastructure (covered by the bill) on a continuous, sector-by-sector basis. The NCCC would also issue regulations establishing risk-based security performance requirements to secure covered critical infrastructure against cyber risks. Each owner or operator of covered critical infrastructure would be required to certify to the NCCC Director that approved security and emergency measures had been implemented. Civil penalties for non-compliance would be established by the bill. The President would be authorized by the bill to declare a national cyber-emergency, and would be required to notify owners and operators of critical infrastructure about the nature of a cyber-threat if a national cyber-emergency was declared.

The Cyber Security Public Awareness Act of 2011[76] (S. 813) is intended to promote the awareness of cybersecurity. Among its provisions, the bill requires a report from be DHS on technical options to enhance the security of information networks of entities which own or manage critical infrastructure. The bill also requires a report from the Secretary of Homeland Security in consultation with the Secretary of Defense and the National Intelligence Director concerning the threat posed by a cyberattack to disrupt the national electrical grid and its implications to national security, the options for quick recovery to provide for national security as well as for restoration of all electrical service in the United States, and the development of a plan to prevent disruption of the U.S. grid by a cyberattack.

---

[74] Introduced in January 2011 by Sen. Reid et al.

[75] Introduced in February 2011 by Sen. Lieberman et al.

[76] Introduced in April 2011 by Senators Whitehouse and Kyl.

House

The National Infrastructure Development Bank Act of 2011[77] (H.R. 402) aims to facilitate infrastructure development. The bill identifies the nation's energy infrastructure as an area in need of modernization. Eligibility is extended to Smart Grid projects as energy infrastructure development.

The Secure High-voltage Infrastructure for Electricity from Lethal Damage Act[78] (H.R. 668) seeks to protect the bulk power system and electric infrastructure critical to the defense and well-being of the United States from EMP threats (such as nuclear weapons), or natural geomagnetic disturbance (GMD) vulnerabilities (such as solar flares). The bill proposes to authorize FERC to order the ERO to take emergency measures to protect the reliability of the bulk power system upon identification of an imminent threat to grid security from an EMP attack or GMD event. FERC would be authorized to allow utilities to recover "substantial costs" incurred from compliance with such an emergency order. The bill would also authorize FERC to issue rules or orders to protect against such grid security vulnerabilities not covered by ERO reliability standards (and would rescind the FERC rule or order when a sufficient ERO reliability standard was in place). FERC would be required to direct the ERO to propose reliability standards to protect against "reasonably foreseeable" EMP or GMD events. The ERO would also be required to propose reliability standards (balancing risks and costs) to address availability of large transformers capable of restoring reliable grid operations after an EMP or GMD event, providing entities (either individually or jointly) which own such transformers to ensure their adequate availability in case such transformers are destroyed or disabled by such an EMP or GMD event. The President would be required to identify up to 100 electric infrastructure facilities critical in supplying power for the defense of the United States which would be subject to FERC rules and orders related to EMP or GMD events. Recovery of full incremental costs incurred in compliance with such FERC rules and orders would be allowed for owners of the identified defense critical electric facilities.

White House Legislative Proposal on Cyberspace

The Obama administration has launched its own comprehensive proposals for legislation on cybersecurity.[79] Protection of critical infrastructure (including the electric grid, financial systems, and transportation networks) is among the main proposals. Other initiatives are suggested to better report cyber-breaches so that consumers are aware that their personal data may have been accessed by intruders, and "synchronized" penalties for cyber-crime with mandatory minimum punishments for cyber-intrusions into critical infrastructure.

The Administration wants better preparedness and coordination between federal agencies, state governments, and industry in order to prevent cyberattacks against critical infrastructure. The proposals include development of cybersecurity standards and enhanced information sharing about cyber threats. The Administration also proposes legislative provisions for DHS to help industry, states, and local government to recover from a cyber-intrusion and fix the resulting damage, or provide advice on building a better network. DHS would also review cyber-protection

---

[77] Introduced in January 2011 by Rep. DeLauro et al.

[78] Introduced in February 2011 by Rep. Franks et al.

[79] White House, Office of the Press Secretary, *Fact Sheet: Cybersecurity Legislative Proposal*, May 12, 2011, http://www.whitehouse.gov/the-press-office/2011/05/12/fact-sheet-cybersecurity-legislative-proposal.

strategies and requirements, making public its findings on readiness (while not revealing the specific nature of any deficiencies).

Additional Comments

Much of the federal efforts related to the cybersecurity of the smarter grid relate to efforts to stay ahead of cyber-threats. But such is the complexity of the cyber-threat universe (with defined threats, perceived weaknesses, and the possibility of continual upgrades of both hardware and software systems) that staying ahead of the threats could quickly evolve into a rapidly growing, never-ending cost center for utilities. While a key to cost control is in assessment of the likely risks, cost recovery for reliability under current federal law is based on mandatory compliance with CIP cybersecurity standards for reliability purposes.

Cost recovery for Smart Grid expenditures or upgrades is voluntary under current law. Such discretionary treatment may possibly result in liability claims if damages result from an attack on Smart Grid systems. While the "Support Anti-Terrorism by Fostering Effective Technologies Act" of 2002[80] provides "risk management" and "litigation management" protection for qualified anti-terrorism technologies and others in the supply and distribution chain, such protections likely do not apply to electric utilities as adopters of Smart Grid technologies and devices.

Current legislative and Administration proposals largely speak to a prioritization of critical infrastructure facilities, with consideration to how these relate to national security, and national economic recovery. However, recoverability from a cyberattack on the scale of something which might take down a significant portion of the grid will likely be very difficult. Maintaining a ready inventory of critical spare parts in close proximity to key installations would likely prove useful to quickening recovery efforts from some types of attack.

The current Smart Grid cybersecurity discussions largely focuses on the security of central station power plants and transmission systems. However, the future Smart Grid may increasingly depend on renewable energy, fuel cells, and other distributed resources like energy storage as these technologies are increasingly integrated into the nation's energy framework. The development of the Smart Grid with distributed and renewable power generation resources may add a level of security to the grid, since these resources do not have the fuel requirements of fossil generation. Damage to the fossil fuel delivery networks would likely impair operation of central station generating plants, depending on how much of an inventory of fuel is stored on-site. This greater diversity of resource options would likely further enhance the Smart Grid's expected improvement in reliability due a greater diversity of resource options, joining together these newer elements with traditional power stations in the power grid of the future. But the characteristics that these elements bring to the system could be considered in the design of CIP standards and protocols.

Although this report has focused on cybersecurity aspects of a smarter electrical grid, technologies being developed for use by the Smart Grid could also be used by natural gas pipeline, water supply, and telecommunications systems. Consideration could be given to applying similar control system device and system safeguards to these other vital utility systems. Consideration could be given to applying similar control system device and system safeguards to

---

[80] P.L. 107-296

these other vital utility systems. The electricity grid is connected to (and largely dependent on) these other resource and communications providers as the vast majority of power production today needs water for steam generation or natural gas for fuel. Similarly, natural gas pipelines use many electrically powered compressors to maintain pipeline pressure and move gas through the system, and the nation's water systems is a notable consumer of electricity for distribution and supply purposes. These interdependent systems are also vulnerable to natural hazards such as earthquakes and tornadoes. The remote sensing and other technologies expected to be employed by the Smart Grid could also help mitigate the effects of regional natural disasters on critical infrastructure, as these are expected to be capable of detecting outages and optimizing power flows to minimize damage and enable a more complete recovery.

Author Contact Information

Richard J. Campbell
Specialist in Energy Policy
rcampbell@crs.loc.gov, 7-7905